D1717038

DIGITAL CITIZENS

SAFETY AND SECURITY

BEN HUBBARD

ILLUSTRATED BY DIEGO VAISBERG

Lerner Publications ◆ Minneapolis

First American edition published in 2019 by
Lerner Publishing Group, Inc.

First published in Great Britain in 2018 by
The Watts Publishing Group
Copyright © The Watts Publishing
Group 2018

Credits
Series Editor: Julia Bird
Illustrator: Diego Vaisberg
Packaged by: Collaborate

Lerner Publications Company
A division of Lerner Publishing Group, Inc.
241 First Avenue North
Minneapolis, MN 55401 USA

For reading levels and more information, look up
this title at www.lernerbooks.com.

Main body text set in Courier PS Std.
Typeface provided by Monotype Typography.

Library of Congress Cataloging-in-Publication Data

Names: Hubbard, Ben, 1973- author. | Vaisberg, Diego, illustrator.
Title: My digital safety and security / by Ben Hubbard ; illustrated
by Diego Vaisberg.
Description: Minneapolis : Lerner Publications, [2019] | Series:
Digital citizens | "First published in Great Britain in 2018 by The
Watts Publishing Group." | Audience: Ages 7-11. | Audience: Grades 4
to 6. | Includes bibliographical references and index.
Identifiers: LCCN 2018033360 (print) | LCCN 2018035251 (ebook) | ISBN
9781541543096 (eb pdf) | ISBN 9781541538825 (lb : alk. paper)
Subjects: LCSH: Computer security—Juvenile literature. | Computer
networks—Security measures—Juvenile literature. | Online social
networks—Security measures—Juvenile literature. | Social media—
Security measures—Juvenile literature. | Privacy, Right of—Juvenile
literature. | Computer crimes—Prevention—Juvenile literature.
Classification: LCC QA76.9.A25 (ebook) | LCC QA76.9.A25 H847 2019
(print) | DDC 005.8—dc23

LC record available at https://lccn.loc.gov/2018033360

Manufactured in the United States of America
1-45065-35892-8/3/2018

CONTENTS

WHAT IS DIGITAL CITIZENSHIP?

When we log onto the internet, we become part of a giant online world.

In this world we can use our smartphones, tablets, and computers to explore, create, and communicate with billions of different people. Together, these people make up a global digital community. That is why they are known as digital citizens. When you use the internet you are a digital citizen too. So what does this mean?

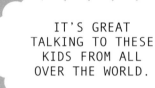

IT'S GREAT TALKING TO THESE KIDS FROM ALL OVER THE WORLD.

CITIZEN VS DIGITAL CITIZEN

A good citizen is someone who behaves well, looks after themselves and others, and tries to make their community a better place. A good digital citizen acts exactly the same way. However, the online world is bigger than just a local neighborhood, city, or country. It spans the whole world and crosses every kind of border. It is therefore up to all digital citizens everywhere to make this digital community a safe, fun, and exciting place for everyone.

MY DIGITAL SAFETY AND SECURITY

Did you know there are over 3.7 billion internet users in the world? Most of these are honest and do not wish others harm. However, just like in the real world, there are some dishonest and dangerous people there too. This is why we need to be prepared and protect ourselves and others around us when we go online. This book will teach you all about staying safe and secure in the digital world.

PREPARE TO PROTECT

Being protected when you go online is not like preparing for battle!

Instead, it's about taking some precautions and then keeping your wits about you while you're there. This means keeping your personal information private, using passwords and passcodes, and being aware of stranger danger. It also means not falling for scams or fake websites and protecting your digital devices against harmful programs and hackers.

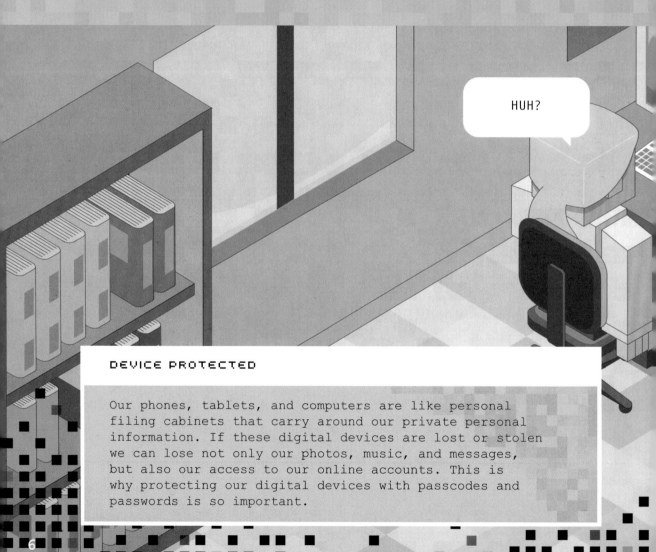

HUH?

DEVICE PROTECTED

Our phones, tablets, and computers are like personal filing cabinets that carry around our private personal information. If these digital devices are lost or stolen we can lose not only our photos, music, and messages, but also our access to our online accounts. This is why protecting our digital devices with passcodes and passwords is so important.

PERSONAL AND PRIVATE

To be safe online, we need to be careful around strangers in the same way we would in the real world. To do this, we must keep personal information about ourselves protected at all times. Smart digital citizens use avatars and screen names for their online accounts and never post their private details, such as telephone numbers and addresses.

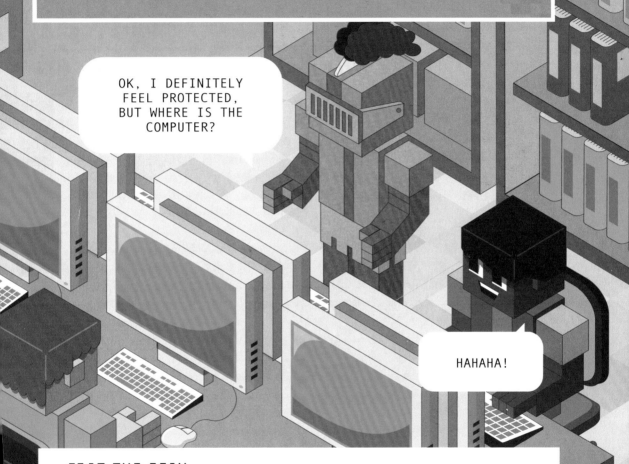

OK, I DEFINITELY FEEL PROTECTED, BUT WHERE IS THE COMPUTER?

HAHAHA!

SPOT THE SCAM

There are many ways people try to scam and steal from others online. Some also wish to damage our digital devices by infecting them with harmful programs such as viruses or malware. Others hack our online accounts to steal our information. These digital dangers can often be avoided by using our common sense and knowing what to look out for.

TRUSTED HELP

It is always a good idea to have a trusted adult around when you go online.

They can help you set up your social media accounts, screen name, and avatar. They can also show you how to navigate the internet and avoid websites that aren't good for kids. Most importantly, your trusted adult is a "go-to" person if something goes wrong.

WHICH ADULT TO CHOOSE?

Choosing the right trusted adult is an important step. It could be a parent, caretaker, or other grown-up family member that lives at home. However, it's best to have a trusted adult that knows more about the online world than you. Otherwise, you will end up being their trusted adult!

NOW, GRANDPA, HOW WILL YOU KEEP ME SAFE ON THE INTERNET?

IS THE INTERNET THAT THING WITH EMAIL?

ONLINE IDENTITY

To avoid giving away too much about yourself, it is best to have a screen name and avatar for your online accounts. A screen name is just a nickname and can be anything you like. Some mix up a favorite singer's name with numbers, for example. An avatar is the online face that you show to the world. Many people copy and paste the face of a movie star or animated character for this.

PROTECTING PERSONAL DETAILS

In the real world we would not go around giving out our personal information to strangers in the street.

The online world is the same. But what does our personal information include? And how do we know what is private and what we can make public?

PERSONAL INFORMATION

Your personal information is made up of the things that identify you. This usually includes your:
- Full name
- Address
- School
- Telephone numbers
- Email address
- Family and friends' personal information

PUBLIC INFORMATION

There is lots of information that doesn't reveal your identity and is safe to give out online. Otherwise you wouldn't be able to say anything! Examples of information that is okay to make public includes your:
- Opinions. It's okay to make your opinions public if you are respectful of others
- Favorite food, singer, or sports team
- How many brothers and sisters you have
- Places you'd like to visit on vacation
- What you'd like to do as a job

PASSWORDS AND PASSCODES

Passwords are how we protect our online accounts, such as email or social media.

This stops anyone else from gaining access and acts as our main line of protection. A second line of protection is a passcode, which is like a password for our digital devices. This means that even if your phone, tablet, or computer is stolen, a thief can't access the information it contains.

PASSCODES

Passcodes are passwords usually made up of numbers that we use to access our digital devices. Without the correct passcode, the device stays on its lock screen. Some digital devices disable completely after a certain number of incorrect guesses. Many phones and tablets now come with a fingerprint scanner instead of a passcode.

PICKING A PASSWORD

A password is a combination of letters, numbers, and special characters that only you know. As a rule, the longer the password, the harder it is to crack. If possible, passwords over 12 characters are best. Try mixing up some different numbers and letters and using uppercase and lowercase letters too. But make sure it is something you will remember! Eight-year-old Jenny has picked this password:

1   Oito
(eight in
Portuguese)

PASSWORDS

A strong password is your best defense against somebody trying to access your online accounts. Websites such as social media sites ask you for a password every time you log in. Only your trusted adult should know what your passwords are, and you must never write them down. It's also important to log out when you have finished, especially if you have used a device other people have access to.

MY CELL PHONE HAS BEEN STOLEN!

DID IT HAVE A PASSCODE PROTECTING IT?

YES, AND I'VE ALREADY BEEN ONLINE TO CHANGE ALL OF MY PASSWORDS ON MY SOCIAL MEDIA ACCOUNTS.

GOOD, THAT'LL HOPEFULLY STOP ANYONE HACKING INTO YOUR ACCOUNTS. NOW LET'S CONTACT YOUR MOBILE PROVIDER AND THE POLICE.

2 MAS (the name of her dog, Sam, backward in capitals)

3 1973 (The year her favorite uncle was born)

4 ****** (six stars for Jenny's age when she got Sam)

5 = OitoMAS1973******

CYBERBULLIES AND TROLLS

Cyberbullies and trolls are internet users that say mean things about others and harass them online.

Often they post nasty comments or photos or send the victim cruel messages. Both trolls and cyberbullies should be taken very seriously so the problem doesn't get worse.

YOUR AVATAR SUCKS. YOU'RE AN IDIOT.

CYBERBULLIES

A cyberbully is often someone we know who has decided to pick on us. It is important to tell your trusted adult right away if you are bullied online. They may choose to get in touch with your school, the website where the abuse is happening, and sometimes the police. Remember that you are not to blame for the bullying.

TROLLS

Online trolls are usually people we don't know who have decided to launch a random attack online. They often wait in forums or chat rooms before making nasty comments and posting rude photographs. Sometimes an attack by a troll can seem silly and like no big deal. But trolling is a form of cyberbullying and should always be reported. After you have done so, it is best to follow the "ignore, block, and unfollow" rule. Trolls usually go away when they do not get attention.

DOXXING

Doxxing is when a cyberbully posts the personal details of their victim so other people can bully them too. This sometimes involves hacking into the victim's online accounts to steal their details. This is why having strong passwords is so important.

PRIVATE SOCIAL MEDIA

Social media websites are where many of us go to connect with our friends and family.

On our social media site we have a webpage "wall" where we can post photos and videos and write up our thoughts in a blog. Others can then comment on what we've done and we can do the same for them. However, we have to be careful about whom we accept as friends.

HUH? WHO ARE YOU? I COULD DO WITH MORE FRIENDS BUT I DON'T KNOW THIS PERSON. DAD?!

PUPPYLOVER23

MEMBERS CLUB

Social media websites are like clubs where you choose who the members are by making them "friends." Then you can access each other's walls and the things you post. New people may "invite" you to become a friend and you can do the same with them. However, you need to be careful whom you accept as friends.

WHO TO SHARE WITH?

You can select the privacy settings on your social media account to choose who sees your wall. The settings usually let you choose "only my friends," "friends of friends," or "everyone." It's best to allow "only my friends" access and block people you do not know. Your trusted adult can help you with these settings.

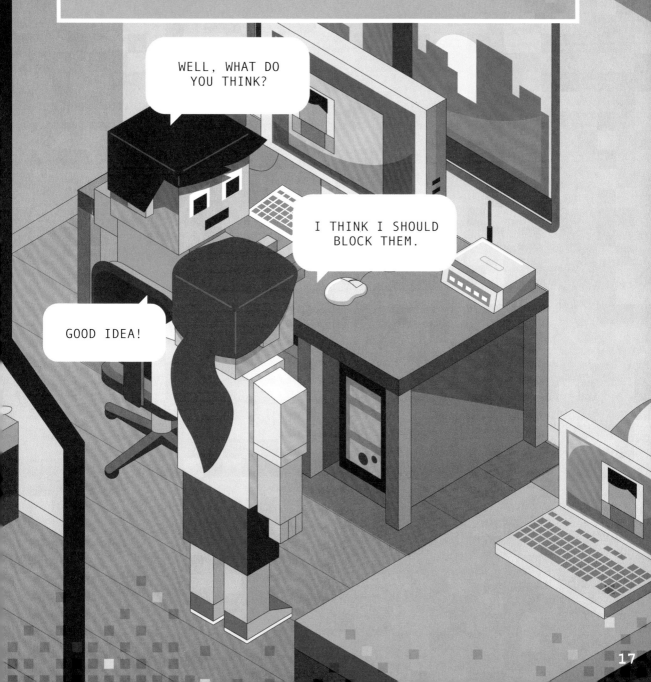

CYBER STRANGERS

Online forums and chat rooms are great places to
meet new people with similar interests as you.

However, unlike social media, everyone in a chat room
is a stranger. This means you need to be extra careful
around the people you meet, even if it feels like you
quickly know them well.

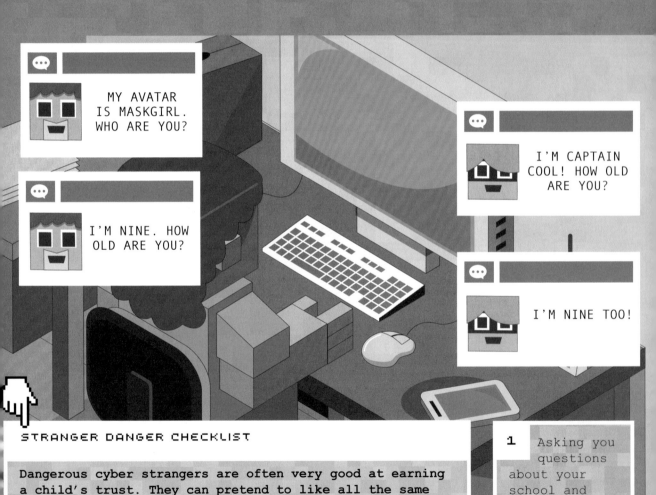

MY AVATAR
IS MASKGIRL.
WHO ARE YOU?

I'M CAPTAIN
COOL! HOW OLD
ARE YOU?

I'M NINE. HOW
OLD ARE YOU?

I'M NINE TOO!

STRANGER DANGER CHECKLIST

Dangerous cyber strangers are often very good at earning
a child's trust. They can pretend to like all the same
things as you and be interested in everything you say.
Soon they can seem like your best friend. But before
long, there will be some telltale signs that should set
off some alarm bells. This is when you must tell your
trusted adult what is going on. These signs can include:

1 Asking you
questions
about your
school and
local area.

WHO ARE YOU REALLY?

Because everyone you meet in an online forum or chat room has an avatar and screen name, you never know for sure who they really are. Someone who claims to be an eight-year-old girl from New York could be a 43-year-old man from London. Sometimes there are dangerous people online who wish to do children harm. That is why it's important not to share any of your personal information.

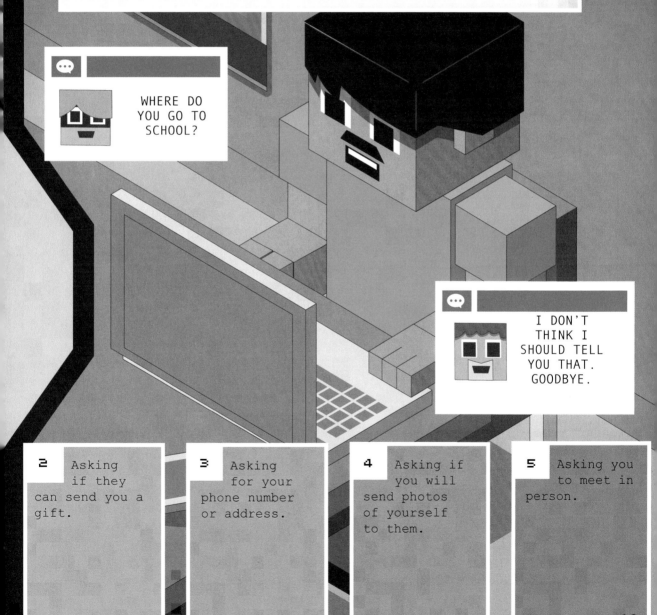

WHERE DO YOU GO TO SCHOOL?

I DON'T THINK I SHOULD TELL YOU THAT. GOODBYE.

2 Asking if they can send you a gift.

3 Asking for your phone number or address.

4 Asking if you will send photos of yourself to them.

5 Asking you to meet in person.

I'M IN TROUBLE

**Even the most careful digital citizens
can sometimes make mistakes online.**
This can include accidentally giving too much away about ourselves
to someone we don't really know. We may have told them some of
our personal information, sent them photos, or made them a promise
we don't want to keep. It's important to remember that it's never
too late to tell your trusted adult if anything like this has
happened. It's also important to never do something you don't want
to do for someone—even if they are putting pressure on you.

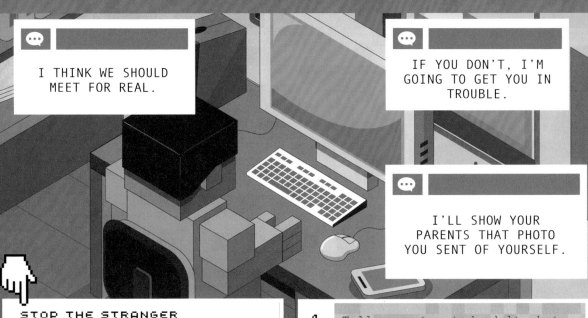

💬

I THINK WE SHOULD
MEET FOR REAL.

💬

IF YOU DON'T, I'M
GOING TO GET YOU IN
TROUBLE.

💬

I'LL SHOW YOUR
PARENTS THAT PHOTO
YOU SENT OF YOURSELF.

STOP THE STRANGER

Dangerous cyber strangers often
pressure their victims and can
even threaten them to get what
they want. If this is happening
to you, remember that you have
the power to stop anything more
from happening. Follow these
steps to make things better:

1 Tell your trusted adult what
has happened. Be honest about
what has taken place—they are
there to help you.

2 If you don't feel like there is a trusted adult you want to tell, you can call a helpline just for kids. Your call will be private and not shared with anyone else.

3 Make a record of all of your correspondence with the stranger, including screen shots. This will help your trusted adult and police investigate. Then block the stranger from all of your accounts.

4 Pat yourself on the back for asking for help. You have done the right thing and started taking back control of your life. Remember that you should never be ashamed to ask for help—regardless of what has happened.

CYBER CRIMINALS

Cyber criminals are dishonest people who make money by scamming and stealing from others online.

Cyber criminals often set a trap on the internet to catch unsuspecting digital citizens. It can be easy to fall into these traps without even realizing, so it's best to stay alert.

MAKE MONEY HERE

Advertisements promising lots of money for little work often catch our attention. Who couldn't do with a bit more pocket money? Sometimes these ads claim to be looking for child "talent" for TV shows or films. However, once you've joined they ask for money for agency "fees." It's simpler not to get sucked in to start with.

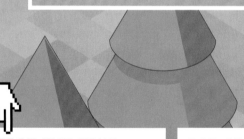

SPOT THE FAKE

It's not always easy to spot a real email or website from a fake. But the following are telltale signs to look out for:

BAD GRAMMAR AND SPELLING

Professional companies have editors that correct mistakes before something is posted online, but cyber criminals do not.

WEIRD-LOOKING LINKS

By resting your mouse (but not clicking) over a link, the real web address is shown. By comparing these, you can see if the link belongs to a fake website.

PHISHING EMAILS AND FAKE WEBSITES

Phishing means being sent an email containing a link that redirects you to a fake website. The website then asks you to download something or to enter your personal details or your credit card number. Your credit card can then be used illegally and the downloaded software can hack your computer and steal your personal information.

DID YOU GET THIS EMAIL FROM SCHOOL ASKING FOR YOUR DETAILS?

NO, THAT DOESN'T SOUND RIGHT. LET'S SEE.

LOOK, THEIR ADDRESS ISN'T QUITE RIGHT, THE EMAIL IS FULL OF SPELLING MISTAKES AND THIS LINK IS DODGY.

THIS IS A PHISHING EMAIL!

NO CONTACT DETAILS

Websites without street addresses and phone numbers are often fakes. You can also check a website's "domain name" online to see if it is trustworthy or not. Your trusted adult can help you with this.

REQUESTS FOR DETAILS

Genuine websites and emails will never ask you for your bank PIN number or any other personal details that could be used to access your private life. Make sure these remain secret.

POP-UPS AND PITFALLS

All digital citizens know that the online world can be a mad maze of pop-up windows, flashing ads, and contest results.

Sometimes it's easy to click on the wrong thing and slip down a blind alleyway. To stay on the right path, beware of the following things.

I'VE WON A NEW PHONE! THEY JUST NEED MY PARENTS' CREDIT CARD DETAILS TO PAY FOR SHIPPING. IT'S WORTH IT!

CONTEST FAKERS

"Congratulations! You've won the latest phone!" When we see online ads such as this, it seems too good to be true. That's because it is. If you click on the window it then asks you for your email address, postal address, and sometimes your credit card number for shipping the prize. But these advertisements are scams, so don't be fooled.

CLICKING THE RIGHT LINK

Often when we are looking to download the latest app or game, we click on the first link we see. But sometimes these downloads are fakes that can unleash harmful viruses or malware. Make sure you only download things from trusted websites that you have used before.

HIDDEN MOBILE CHARGES

Have you ever had a pop-up window on your phone wanting to predict your future or tell you which Star Wars character you are like? All that is needed is your smartphone number. However, by doing this and agreeing to the terms, you will almost certainly be charged a one-time fee. It's better to click away.

DO YOU KNOW ANYTHING ABOUT ALL THESE CREDIT CARD PURCHASES?

SOMEONE'S RIPPED US OFF. AND MY PHONE NEVER ARRIVED!

ACCIDENTAL SPENDING

It's easy to spend money online by accident. Some gaming apps are free to download but charge to access a certain level. If your family uses an online store often and have their credit card details saved there, you can easily make a purchase by clicking on the wrong button. Use your common sense and read the terms and conditions to avoid these spending pitfalls.

VIRUSES AND MALWARE

Digital citizens have to protect their online accounts from cyber criminals and online scams, but they also have to protect their digital devices too.

This means preventing them being infected by harmful malware and viruses.

THAT WAS A NICE THOUGHT. THANKS FOR THE E-CARD.

WAIT . . . I DIDN'T SEND YOU ONE. DON'T OPEN IT!

VIRUSES AND MALWARE

Some of the main programs that can harm your digital devices are:

1 Malware: short for MALicious SoftWARE, malware is designed to damage your device or steal the information on it.

STAY PROTECTED

The simplest defense against viruses and malware is not to click on any suspicious links or email attachments. You can create another line of defense by keeping your anti-virus software up to date. This is designed to stop dangerous programs from entering your digital device in the first place. Leaving your firewall switched on is also important. This is a security shield that stops scammers from getting into your digital device.

FIENDISH FRIENDS?

Sometimes an email containing malware can be sent from a friend or family member's hacked account. These can come with attachments such as a greeting e-card that contains harmful malware. Be cautious of any emails with attachments and look out for spelling mistakes and anything else that looks fishy.

2 Virus: harmful malware that installs itself in the programs already on your digital device and spreads itself to other computers via the internet.

3 Spyware: malware that collects information about you from your digital device.

4 Trojan Horse: a program that gives someone secret access to your digital device, usually to steal from it.

DIGITAL QUIZ

Now that you've reached the end of this book, how do you feel about your digital safety and security?

How much have you learned? And how much can you remember? Take this quiz and tally up your score at the end to find out.

1. Which of these things keep you protected online?
a. A suit of armor
b. An avatar and screen name
c. A filing cabinet

2. Which of these are examples of private information?
a. Your favorite color, football team, and food
b. The number of pets you have
c. Your phone number and address

3. Which of these would be considered a "strong" password?
a. 123456789
b. Password
c. £DinnerTRAIN791;-(

4. Which of these is someone that attacks people online?
a. Troll
b. Poll
c. Moll

5. What should you do if a cyber stranger asks for your address?
a. Give them a fake address
b. Give them your cousin's address
c. Tell your trusted adult

6. Which of these social media privacy settings is best?
a. Only my friends
b. Friends of friends
c. Everyone

7. How can you sometimes spot a fake email?

a. It has lots of spelling mistakes

b. It has "fake" in the subject line

c. It promises that it is not lying

8. What should you never enter online without permission?

a. Numbers between 10 and 15

b. A hidden spacecraft

c. Your parent's credit card details

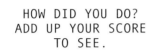

HOW DID YOU DO? ADD UP YOUR SCORE TO SEE.

1-4: You are on your way, but retake the quiz to get a score over 4.

5-7: You've passed the quiz well. Now see if you can pass the quiz in the book *My Digital Health and Wellness*.

8: Wow! 8 out of 8. You are a natural born digital citizen!

ANSWERS

1: b; 2: c; 3: c; 4: a; 5: c; 6: c; 7: a; 8: c

GLOSSARY

apps
Short for "applications," apps are computer programs for mobile digital devices, such as smartphones or tablets

attachment
A file, such as a picture or word document, sent as part of an email

avatar
A computer icon or image that people use to represent themselves online

block
A way of stopping someone from sending you nasty messages, emails, or texts online

cyberbullying
Bullying that takes place online or using internet-based apps

digital
Technology that involves computers

download
To take information or files from the internet and store them on your computer

hacker
A computer expert who breaks into computers and computer networks online

internet
The vast electronic network that allows billions of computers from around the world to connect to each other

malware
A dangerous computer program that is created to damage or disable other digital devices

online
Being connected to the internet via a computer or digital device

privacy settings
Controls on social media websites that allow you decide who has access to your profile and posts

smartphone
A cell phone that is capable of connecting to the internet

social media
Websites that allow users to share content and information online

trusted adult
An adult you know well and trust who can help you with all issues relating to the internet

website
A collection of web pages that is stored on a computer and made available to people over the internet

HELPFUL WEBSITES

Digital Citizenship
The following websites have helpful information about digital citizenship for young people:

http://www.digizen.org/kids/

http://www.digitalcitizenship.nsw.edu.au/Prim_Splash/

http://www.cyberwise.org/digital-citizenship-games

Bullying
These websites have excellent advice for kids who are experiencing bullying online:

https://www.childline.org.uk/info-advice/bullying-abuse-safety/types-bullying/online-bullying/

http://www.bullying.co.uk

https://www.stopbullying.gov/kids/facts

Staying Safe
These websites are dedicated to keeping kids safe online, with lots of good advice:

http://www.childnet.com/young-people/primary

http://www.kidsmart.org.uk

http://www.safetynetkids.org.uk/personal-safety/staying-safe-online/

http://www.bbc.co.uk/newsround/13910067

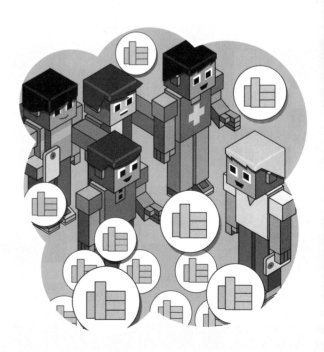

INDEX

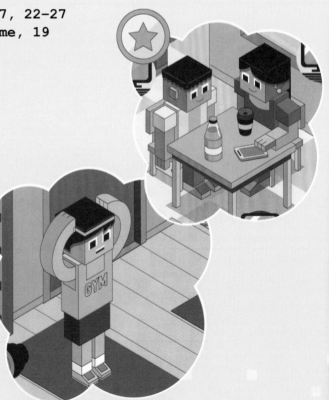